THE
CIVIL
WAR

THE CIVIL WAR

EDITED BY
JASON SHATTUCK

Britannica®
Educational Publishing

IN ASSOCIATION WITH

ROSEN
EDUCATIONAL SERVICES

Published in 2016 by Britannica Educational Publishing (a trademark of Encyclopædia Britannica, Inc.) in association with The Rosen Publishing Group, Inc.
29 East 21st Street, New York, NY 10010

Distributed exclusively by Rosen Publishing.
To see additional Britannica Educational Publishing titles, go to rosenpublishing.com.

First Edition

Britannica Educational Publishing
J.E. Luebering: Director, Core Reference Group
Anthony L. Green: Editor, Compton's by Britannica

Rosen Publishing
Nelson Sá: Art Director
Michael Moy: Designer
Cindy Reiman: Photography Manager
Karen Huang: Photo Researcher
Introduction and supplementary material by Jason Shattuck

Library of Congress Cataloging-in-Publication Data

The Civil War / edited by Jason Shattuck. — First edition.
     pages cm. — (Early American history)
 Includes bibliographical references and index.
 ISBN 978-1-68048-272-0 (library bound)
 1. United States—History—Civil War, 1861-1865—Juvenile literature. I. Shattuck, Jason.
 E468.C615 2016
 973.7--dc23

2015025840

Manufactured in the United States of America

CONTENTS

INTRODUCTION...6

CHAPTER ONE
FORCES AND STRATEGIES
OF THE NORTH AND SOUTH....................10

CHAPTER TWO
THE WAR IN 1861–62................................18

CHAPTER THREE
THE WAR IN 1863................................39

CHAPTER FOUR
THE WAR IN 1864–65................................53

CONCLUSION..64

TIMELINE..67

GLOSSARY...71

FOR MORE INFORMATION...73

BIBLIOGRAPHY..76

INDEX..78

INTRODUCTION

At 4:30 AM on April 12, 1861, Confederate artillery in Charleston, South Carolina, opened fire on Fort Sumter, which was held by the United States Army. The bombardment set off a savage four-year war between two great geographic sections of the United States. One section was the North—23 Northern and Western states that supported the federal government. The other section was the South—11 Southern states that had seceded (withdrawn) from the Union and formed an independent government called the Confederate States of America. The struggle between these two combatants is generally known as the American Civil War, although it sometimes is also referred to as the War Between the States.

The secession of the Southern states (in chronological order, South Carolina, Mississippi, Florida, Alabama, Georgia, Louisiana, Texas, Virginia, Arkansas, North Carolina, and Tennessee) in 1860–61 and the ensuing outbreak of armed conflict were the climax of decades of growing sectional friction over slavery. Between 1815 and 1861 the economy of the Northern states was rapidly modernizing and diversifying. Although agriculture—mostly smaller farms that relied on free labor—remained the dominant sector in the North, industrialization had taken root there. Moreover, Northerners had invested

A map of the major battles of the Civil War shows that most of the battles took place in the Southern states. Many people today see the war as the central event of American history.

heavily in an expansive and varied transportation system that included canals, roads, steamboats, and railroads. They had also put money into financial industries such as banking and insurance and in a large communications network that featured inexpensive, widely available newspapers, magazines, and books, along with the telegraph.

By contrast, the Southern economy was based principally on large farms (plantations) that produced commercial crops such as cotton and that relied on slaves as the main labor force. Rather than invest in factories or railroads as Northerners had done, Southerners invested their money in slaves—even more than in land. By 1860, 84 percent of the capital invested in manufacturing was invested in the free (nonslave-holding) states. Yet, to Southerners, as late as 1860, this appeared to be a sound business decision. The price of cotton, the South's defining crop, had skyrocketed in the 1850s, and the value of slaves—who were, after all, property—rose correspondingly. By 1860 the per capita wealth of Southern whites was twice that of Northerners, and three-fifths of the wealthiest individuals in the country were Southerners.

The extension of slavery into new territories and states had been an issue as far back as the Northwest Ordinance of 1784. When the slave territory of Missouri sought statehood in 1818, Congress debated for two years before arriving at the Missouri Compromise of 1820. This was the first of a series of political deals that resulted from arguments between proslavery and antislavery forces over the expansion of the "peculiar institution," as it was known, into the West. The end of the Mexican-American War in 1848 and the roughly 500,000 square miles (1.3 million square kilometers) of new territory that the United States gained as a result of it added a new sense of urgency to the dispute. More and more Northerners, driven by a sense of morality or an interest in protecting free labor, came to believe, in the 1850s, that bondage needed to be abolished. White Southerners feared that limiting the expansion of slavery would deliver the institution to certain death. Over the course of the decade, the two sides became increasingly polarized and politicians less able to contain the dispute through compromise. When Abraham Lincoln, the candidate of the antislavery Republican Party, won the 1860 presidential election, seven Southern states (South Carolina, Mississippi, Florida, Alabama, Georgia, Louisiana, and Texas) carried out their threat and seceded, organizing as the Confederate States of America.

The Civil War focuses primarily on the war itself—its major battles, campaigns, and military leaders—and the cost and significance of the conflict.

CHAPTER ONE

FORCES AND STRATEGIES OF THE NORTH AND SOUTH

I n the early morning hours of April 12, 1861, Confederate rebels opened fire on Fort Sumter, at the entrance to the harbor of Charleston, South Carolina. Curiously, this first encounter of what would be the bloodiest war in the history of the United States claimed no victims. After a 34-hour bombardment, Major Robert Anderson surrendered his command of about 85 soldiers to some 5,500 besieging Confederate troops under P.G.T. Beauregard, a brigadier general.

With war upon the land, President Abraham Lincoln called for 75,000 militiamen to serve for three months. He proclaimed a naval blockade of the Confederate states, although he insisted that they did not legally constitute a sovereign country but were instead states

Photographer Mathew Brady took this picture of the Company "A" 9th Indiana Infantry. At the start of the Civil War, President Abraham Lincoln called for loyal states to furnish state militiamen to help defend the Union.

in rebellion. Lincoln also directed the secretary of the treasury to advance $2 million to assist in the raising of troops, and he suspended the writ of habeas corpus, first along the East Coast and ultimately throughout the country. The Confederate government had previously authorized a call for 100,000 soldiers for at least six months' service, and this figure was soon increased to 400,000.

COMPARISON OF NORTH AND SOUTH

At first glance it seemed that the 23 states that remained in the Union after secession were more than a match for the 11 Southern states. About 21 million people lived in the North, compared with some nine million in the South of whom about four million were slaves. In addition, the North was the site of more than 100,000 manufacturing plants, against 18,000 south of the Potomac River, and more than 70 percent of the railroads were in the Union. Furthermore, the Union had at its command a 30-to-1 superiority in arms production, a 2-to-1 edge in available manpower, and a greater number of commercial and financial resources. The Union also had a functioning government and a small but efficient regular army and navy.

The Confederacy was not predestined to defeat, however. The Southern armies had the advantage of fighting on interior lines, and their military tradition had been significant in the history of the United States before 1860. Moreover, the long Confederate coastline of 3,500 miles (5,600 kilometers) seemed to defy blockade, and the Confederate president, Jefferson Davis, hoped to receive decisive foreign aid and intervention. Confederate soldiers were fighting to achieve a separate and independent country based on what they called "Southern institutions," the chief of which was the institution of slavery. So the Southern cause was not a lost one; indeed, other countries—most notably

Jefferson Davis was the president and commander in chief of the Confederacy.

the United States itself in the American Revolution (1775–83) against Great Britain—had won independence against equally heavy odds.

In the beginning both sides tried to raise troops only on a volunteer basis, but they soon found it necessary to adopt a military draft. The South resorted to conscription in 1862, and the North did the following year. Both sides also had great difficulty in equipping their troops. It was many months before Northern factories were producing enough goods for the Union armies. The South, with few industrial resources, had to import much of its equipment from Europe, running it through the naval blockade imposed by Union vessels.

THE COMMANDERS IN CHIEF

Of the two rival commanders in chief, most people in 1861 thought Jefferson Davis to be abler than Abraham Lincoln. Davis was a graduate of the U.S. Military Academy, a hero of the Mexican-American War, a capable secretary of war under President Franklin Pierce, and a U.S. representative and senator from Mississippi. Lincoln—who had served in the Illinois state legislature and as an undistinguished one-term member of the U.S. House of Representatives—could boast of only a brief period of military service in the Black Hawk War, in which he saw no action.

As president and commander in chief of the Confederate forces, Davis revealed many fine qualities, including dignity, firmness, determination, and honesty, but he was flawed by his excessive pride, hypersensitivity to criticism, poor political skills, and tendency to micromanage. He engaged in petty quarrels with generals and cabinet members. He also suffered from ill health throughout the conflict. To a large extent and by his own preference, Davis was his own secretary of war, although five different men served in that post during the lifetime of the Confederacy. Davis himself also filled the position of general in chief of the Confederate armies until he named Robert E. Lee to that position in 1865, near the end of the war.

To the astonishment of many, Lincoln grew in stature with time and experience, and by 1864 he had become a consummate politician and war director. Lincoln matured into a remarkably effective president because of his great intelligence, communication skills, humility, sense of purpose, sense of humor, fundamentally moderate nature, and ability to remain focused on the big picture. But he had much to learn at first, especially in strategic and tactical matters and in his choices of army commanders. With an ineffective first secretary of war–Simon Cameron–Lincoln involved himself directly in the planning of military movements. Edwin M. Stanton, a well-known lawyer appointed as secretary of war on January 20, 1862, was equally untutored in military affairs, but he was fully as active a participant as his superior.

STRATEGIC PLANS

In the area of grand strategy, Davis persistently adhered to the defensive, permitting only occasional "spoiling" forays into Northern territory. Perhaps the Confederates' best chance of winning would have been an early grand offensive into the Union states before the Lincoln administration could find its ablest

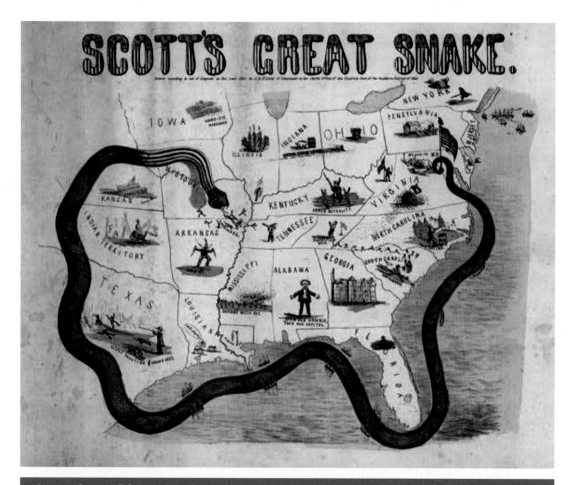

A map from 1861 shows General Winfield Scott's Anaconda Plan, a military strategy that called for a naval blockade of the South's coastline and a Union drive down the Mississippi to control it and thus help strangle the Confederacy, much like an anaconda does to its prey.

generals and bring the superior resources of the North to bear against the South. On the other hand, protecting the territory the Confederacy already controlled was of paramount importance, and a defensive position allowed the rebels to economize their resources somewhat better.

To crush the rebellion and reestablish the authority of the federal government, Lincoln had to direct his armies to invade, capture, and hold most of the vital areas of the Confederacy. His grand strategy was based on the so-called Anaconda Plan devised by Winfield Scott, the first general in chief of the Union forces. It called for a Union blockade of the Confederacy's coastline as well as a decisive thrust down the Mississippi River and an ensuing strangulation of the South by Union land and naval forces. But it was to take four years of grim, unrelenting warfare and enormous casualties and devastation before the Confederates could be defeated and the Union preserved.

CHAPTER TWO

THE WAR IN 1861–62

During 1861 both the North and South hastened to create field armies. After the initial encounter at Fort Sumter, the next battles took place in Virginia. Throughout the remainder of the year, the fighting remained concentrated in the border states. By the end of 1861, however, two major battlefronts had developed. One was in the East where Virginia, Maryland, and Pennsylvania suffered the bulk of the fighting. The other front was in the West, at first along the Mississippi River.

THE FIRST YEAR OF WAR

In northwestern Virginia, nonslaveholding pro-Union Virginians sought to secede from the Confederacy. George B. McClellan, in command of Union forces

Early on April 12, 1861, Confederate forces fired on Fort Sumter in Charleston's harbor. The Confederate states claimed control of all forts within their borders, but President Abraham Lincoln refused to order U.S. troops to leave them.

in southern Ohio, advanced on his own initiative in the early summer of 1861 into western Virginia with about 20,000 men. He encountered smaller forces sent there by General Robert E. Lee, who was then in Richmond in command of all Virginia troops.

Although showing signs of occasional hesitation, McClellan quickly won three small but significant battles: on June 3 at Philippi, on July 11 at Rich Mountain, and on July 13 at Carrick's (or Corrick's) Ford (all now in West Virginia). McClellan's casualties were light, and his victories went far toward eliminating Confederate resistance in northwestern Virginia, which had refused to recognize secession, and toward paving the way for the admittance into the Union of the new state of West Virginia in 1863.

Meanwhile, sizable armies were gathering around the federal capital of Washington, D.C., and the Confederate capital of Richmond, Virginia, which was about 100 miles (160 kilometers) south of Washington. Union forces abandoned positions in Virginia, including, on April 18, Harpers Ferry (now in West Virginia), which was quickly occupied by Southern forces, who held it for a time, and the naval base at Norfolk, which was prematurely abandoned to the Confederacy on April 20. On May 6 Lee ordered a Confederate force—soon to be commanded by P.G.T. Beauregard—northward to hold the rail hub of Manassas Junction, Virginia, some 26 miles (42 kilometers) southwest of Washington. With Lincoln's approval, Scott appointed Irvin McDowell to command the main Union army that was being hastily collected near Washington. But political pressure and Northern public opinion impelled Lincoln, against Scott's advice, to order McDowell's still-untrained army to push the Confederates back from Manassas. Meanwhile, Union forces were to hold Confederate soldiers under Joseph E. Johnston in the Shenandoah Valley near Winchester, Virginia, thus preventing them from reinforcing Beauregard along the Bull Run, a small river near Manassas.

McDowell advanced from Washington on July 16 with some 32,000 men and moved slowly toward Bull Run. Two days later a reconnaissance in force (an attack by a large force to determine the size and strength of the enemy) was repulsed by the Confederates at Mitchell's Ford and Blackburn's Ford. When McDowell attacked on July 21 in the First Battle of Bull Run (which came to be known in the South as First Manassas), he discovered that Johnston had escaped the Union forces in the valley and had joined Beauregard near Manassas just in time, bringing the total Confederate force to around 28,000. McDowell's sharp attacks with inexperienced troops forced the equally untrained Southerners back a bit, but a strong defensive stand by Thomas Jonathan Jackson (who thereby gained the nickname "Stonewall") enabled the Confederates to check and finally throw back the Union troops in the afternoon. The Union retreat to Washington soon became a rout. McDowell lost 2,708 men—killed, wounded, and missing—against a Southern loss of 1,981. Both sides now settled down to a long war, but the First Battle of Bull Run left a lasting impression on both

In the First Battle of Bull Run (First Manassas), Union troops initially seemed to be in control, but when Confederate forces were reinforced, the Northerners retreated. Confederate General Thomas Jackson stood firm, earning him the nickname Stonewall Jackson.

the Confederacy and the Union. The Confederates took their victory as confirmation of their belief that a single rebel soldier was worth 10 Union soldiers, an overconfident and dangerously unrealistic mindset. On the Union side, the loss seems to have infected the high command of the Army of the Potomac—the main Union army in the East—with both an inferiority complex and a wary fear of Southern military proficiency. This attitude was in evidence until Ulysses S. Grant became the general in charge of all the armies in the spring of 1864.

THE EAST IN 1862

Fresh from his victories in western Virginia, McClellan was called to Washington to replace Scott. There he began to mold the Army of the Potomac into a resolute, effective shield and sword of the Union. But personality clashes and unrelenting opposition to McClellan from the Radical Republicans in Congress hampered the sometimes tactless general, who was a Democrat. It took time to drill, discipline, and equip this force of considerably more than 100,000 men, but, as fall blended into winter, loud demands arose that McClellan advance against Johnston's Confederate forces at Centreville and Manassas in Virginia. McClellan fell seriously ill with typhoid fever in December, and when he had recovered weeks later he found that Lincoln, desperately eager for action, had ordered him to advance on February 22, 1862. Long debates ensued between president and commander. These disagreements led McClellan to make state-ments and take actions that would have been—and indeed were—considered insubordinate by almost anyone other than the extremely patient Lincoln. When in March McClellan finally began his Peninsular Campaign, he discovered that Lincoln and Stanton had withheld large numbers of his command in front of Washington for the defense of the capital—forces that actually were not needed there. Upon taking command of the army in the field, McClellan was relieved of his duties as general in chief.

THE PENINSULAR CAMPAIGN

Advancing up the historic peninsula between the York and James rivers in Virginia, McClellan began a month-long siege of Yorktown and captured that stronghold

THE FIRST BATTLES OF THE IRONCLADS

The naval side of the Civil War was a revolutionary one. In addition to their increasing use of steam power, the screw propeller, shell guns, and rifled ordnance, both sides built and employed ironclad warships.

On the afternoon of March 8, 1862, five vessels of the United States Navy lay at anchor in Hampton Roads, Virginia. Suddenly a strange-looking object moved through the water toward the U.S. vessel *Cumberland* from the Confederate stronghold in Norfolk, Virginia. It was a reconstructed U.S. ship, the *Merrimack* (renamed the *Virginia*). The vessel had been sunk when the Norfolk navy yard was abandoned at the beginning of the war. The Confederates had raised the vessel, cut off the sides, and covered what was left with iron plates. This under-taking was one of the earliest practical applications of armor to a warship.

The ironclad steered straight for the *Cumberland*. It was met by heavy fire, but, when it reached the *Cumberland*, its iron beak cut through the side of the wooden vessel "as a knife goes through cheese." The *Merrimack* next set fire to the *Congress* with red-hot shot from its guns. Then the vessel steamed away to pre-pare for its next victory.

By the next morning, however, the situation was entirely changed. When the *Merrimack* started toward the *Minnesota*, preparing to dispose of it as quickly as the two victims of the previous day, there suddenly appeared

CONTINUED ON THE NEXT PAGE

CONTINUED FROM THE PREVIOUS PAGE

The *Merrimack* and the *Monitor*, two ironclad ships, clash on March 9, 1862. Also called the Battle of Hampton Roads, it was the first duel between ironclads. The battle ended in a draw.

in the ironclad's path an odd object, about one-fourth the *Merrimack*'s size and resembling a "cheese-box on a raft." This was the famous *Monitor*, a Union ironclad designed by John Ericsson, a Swedish engineer.

The fight between the two ships began at once and lasted for nearly four hours. The *Monitor* was more easily handled than the *Merrimack*, but its shots could not do much harm to the other's iron sides. On the other hand, the *Monitor*'s single revolving turret offered a hopeless target for its opponent. Thousands of people stood on the shore and breathlessly watched the combat. The distance between the vessels varied from half a mile to a few yards. The *Monitor*'s commander was wounded, and the *Merrimack*, badly damaged, steamed back to Norfolk.

This fight between the *Merrimack* and *Monitor* was one of the most important naval battles ever fought, for it made the warships of all the old navies useless. All countries had to discard their wooden vessels and to begin building ironclads. During the Civil War the Union was able to build more iron ships faster than the Confederacy could.

on May 4, 1862. A Confederate rearguard action at Williamsburg the next day delayed the Union troops, who then slowly moved up through heavy rain to within 4 miles (6 kilometers) of Richmond. Striving to seize the initiative, Johnston attacked McClellan's left wing at Seven Pines (Fair Oaks) on May 31 and, after scoring initial gains, was checked. Johnston was severely wounded, and, in a major though often overlooked development of the war, Lee, who had been serving as Davis's military adviser, succeeded him. Lee promptly renamed the command the Army of Northern Virginia. McClellan counterattacked on June 1 and forced the Southerners back into the environs of Richmond. The North suffered a total of 5,031 casualties out of a force of nearly 100,000, while the Confederates lost 6,134 of about 74,000 men.

As McClellan inched forward toward Richmond in June, Lee prepared a counterstroke. He recalled from the Shenandoah Valley Jackson's forces—which had threatened Harpers Ferry and had brilliantly defeated several scattered Union armies—and, with about 90,000 soldiers, attacked McClellan on June 26 to begin the fighting of the Seven Days' Battles (usually dated June 25–July 1). In the ensuing days at Mechanicsville, Gaines's Mill, Savage's Station, Frayser's Farm (Glendale), and Malvern Hill, Lee tried unsuccessfully to crush the Army of the Potomac, which McClellan was moving to another base on the James River, but the Confederate commander had at least saved Richmond. McClellan inflicted 20,614 casualties on Lee while suffering 15,849 himself. McClellan felt that he could not move upon Richmond without considerable reinforcement, and his estimates of the men he needed went up and up and up. Against his protests his army was withdrawn from the peninsula to Washington by Lincoln and the new general in chief, Henry Halleck—a man McClellan scornfully considered to be his inferior. Many of McClellan's units were given to a new Union army commander, John Pope, who was directed to move overland against Richmond.

SECOND BATTLE OF BULL RUN (MANASSAS) AND ANTIETAM

General Pope advanced confidently toward the Rappahannock River with his Army of Virginia while Lee, once McClellan had been pulled back from near Richmond, moved northward to confront Pope before he could be joined by all of McClellan's troops. Daringly splitting his army, Lee sent Jackson to destroy Pope's base at Manassas, while he himself advanced via another route with James Longstreet's half of the army. Pope opened the Second Battle of Bull Run (in the South, Second Manassas) on August 29 with heavy but futile attacks on Jackson. The next day Lee arrived and crushed the Union left with a massive flank assault by Longstreet, which, combined with Jackson's counterattacks, drove the Northerners back in rout upon Washington. Pope lost 16,054 men out of a force of

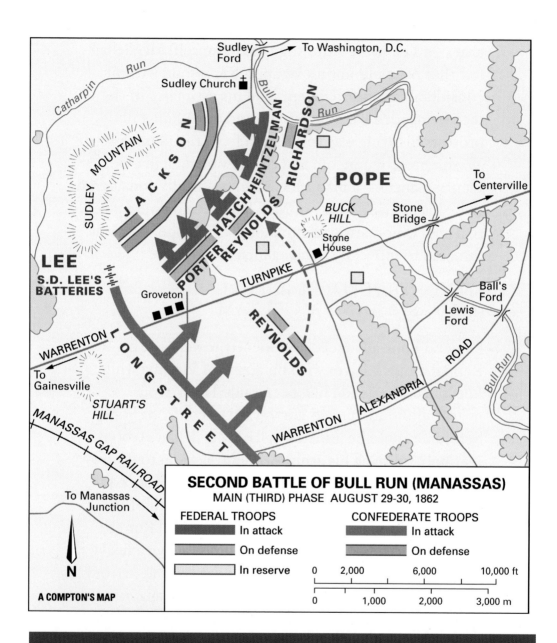

SECOND BATTLE OF BULL RUN (MANASSAS)
MAIN (THIRD) PHASE AUGUST 29-30, 1862

FEDERAL TROOPS

	In attack
	On defense
	In reserve

CONFEDERATE TROOPS

	In attack
	On defense

0	2,000		6,000	10,000 ft
0		1,000	2,000	3,000 m

N

A COMPTON'S MAP

A map depicts Union and Confederate positions in the Second Battle of Bull Run (Second Manassas) on August 29–30, 1862. Confederate troops under General Robert E. Lee defeated Union forces under General John Pope.

about 70,000, while Lee lost 9,197 out of about 55,000. With the Union soldiers now lacking confidence in Pope, Lincoln relieved him and merged his forces into McClellan's Army of the Potomac.

Lee followed up his advantage with his first invasion of the North, pushing as far as Frederick, Maryland. His hope was to bring Maryland (a slave state that

THE EMANCIPATION PROCLAMATION

The Union victory at Antietam, slight though it was, gave President Lincoln the opportunity to issue the Emancipation Proclamation. This order decreed the freedom of all slaves in territory still in rebellion on January 1, 1863. The president took this momentous step to introduce a new moral aim in the war and to prevent foreign intervention.

The Emancipation Proclamation also allowed black men to serve in the Union army. This had been illegal under a federal law enacted in 1792 (although African Americans had served in the army in the War of 1812 and the law had never applied to the navy). With their stake in the Civil War now patently obvious, African Americans joined the service in significant numbers. By the end of the war, about 180,000 African Americans were in the army, which amounted to about 10 percent of the troops in that branch, and another 20,000 were serving in the navy.

had remained in the Union) into the Confederacy. He also felt that if he could continue to grind down civilian will on the Union side, the North would grant the Confederacy its independence. McClellan had to reorganize his army on the march, a task that he performed capably. But McClellan could not overcome his own worst impulses. He overestimated the size of Lee's army by a factor of about two and a half. Worse, he failed to capitalize on an astonishing stroke of luck: the capture of Lee's orders, discovered on the ground wrapped around three cigars. Rather than striking immediately against Lee's scattered forces, McClellan waited 18 hours before moving. Finally, McClellan pressed forward and wrested the initiative from Lee by attacking and defeating a Confederate force at three gaps of the South Mountain between Frederick and Hagerstown on September 14.

Lee fell back into a cramped defensive position along Antietam Creek, near Sharpsburg, Maryland. There he was reinforced by Jackson, who had just captured about 11,500 Union soldiers at Harpers Ferry. After yet another delay, McClellan struck the Confederates on September 17 in the bloodiest day of the war. Although gaining some ground, the Northerners were unable to drive the Confederate army into the Potomac, but Lee was compelled to retreat back into Virginia. At Antietam, McClellan lost 12,410 of some 69,000 engaged, while Lee lost 13,724 of perhaps 52,000. When McClellan did not pursue Lee as quickly as Lincoln and Halleck

Alexander Gardner, a photographer with Mathew Brady's studio, took this picture of Confederate dead along the Hagerstown road in Antietam, Maryland, in September 1862. The Battle of Antietam was one of the costliest of the Civil War.

thought he should, he was replaced in command by Ambrose E. Burnside, an assistant of McClellan who had been an ineffective corps commander at Antietam.

FREDERICKSBURG

General Burnside delayed for a number of weeks before marching his reinforced army of 120,281 men to a point across the Rappahannock River from Fredericksburg, Virginia. On December 13 he ordered a series of 16 hopeless, piecemeal frontal assaults across open ground against Lee's army of 78,513 troops, drawn up in an impregnable position atop high ground and behind a stone wall. The Union forces were repelled with staggering losses. "If there is a worse place than hell, I am in it," Lincoln reportedly said.

Morale in the Army of the Potomac fell further in January, when Burnside ordered a flanking maneuver against rebel forces. After an auspicious start to the march on January 20, 1863, a driving rain began that night. The Northerners quickly bogged down in what became known as the "Mud March." Burnside turned back on January 23. As Union confidence plunged, desertions rose. On January 25, 1863, Lincoln replaced Burnside with a proficient corps commander, Joseph ("Fighting Joe") Hooker, who was a harsh critic of other generals and even of the president. Both armies went into winter quarters near Fredericksburg.

THE WAR IN THE WEST

Meanwhile, Union and Confederate forces were battling in the Western theater. Throughout the war, Union campaigns were more successful in the West.

African American soldiers liberate slaves in North Carolina in 1864. After President Lincoln issued the Emancipation Proclamation in 1863, many freed African Americans enlisted in the Union army and navy.

MISSOURI

In the vital Mississippi Valley, operations were unfolding as large and as important as those on the Atlantic seaboard. Missouri and Kentucky were key border states that President Lincoln had to retain within the Union orbit. Commanders there—especially on the Union side—had greater autonomy than those in Virginia. Affairs began inauspiciously for the Union in Missouri when Nathaniel Lyon's 5,000 troops were defeated at Wilson's Creek on August 10, 1861, by a Confederate force of more than 10,000 under Sterling Price and Benjamin McCulloch, each side losing some 1,200 men. But Union forces under Samuel Curtis decisively set back a Southern army under Earl Van Dorn at Pea Ridge (Elkhorn Tavern), Arkansas, on March 7–8, 1862, saving Missouri for the Union and threatening Arkansas.

KENTUCKY AND TENNESSEE

The Confederates to the east of Missouri had established a unified command under Albert Sidney Johnston, who manned, with only 40,000 men, a long line in Kentucky running from near Cumberland Gap on the east through Bowling Green to Columbus on the Mississippi River. Numerically superior Union forces cracked this line in early 1862. First, George H. Thomas broke Johnston's right flank at Mill Springs (Somerset), Kentucky, on January 19. Then, in February, Ulysses S. Grant, assisted by Union gunboats commanded by Andrew H. Foote and acting under Halleck's orders, ruptured the center of the Southern line in Kentucky by capturing Fort Henry on the Tennessee River and Fort Donelson, 11 miles (18 kilometers) to the east, on the Cumberland River (both forts located in Tennessee). The Confederates suffered more than 16,000 casualties at the latter stronghold—most of them taken prisoner—against Union losses of fewer than 3,000, and Grant's victories at Forts Henry and Donelson marked the first real successes for the Union in the war. Johnston's left anchor fell when Pope seized New Madrid, Missouri, and Island Number Ten in the Mississippi River in March and April. This Union advance forced Johnston to withdraw his remnants quickly from Kentucky through Tennessee and to reorganize them for a counterstroke. This seemingly impossible task he performed splendidly.

The Confederate onslaught came at Shiloh, Tennessee, near Pittsburg Landing, a point on the west bank of the Tennessee River to which Union Generals Grant and William T. Sherman had incautiously advanced. The Battle of Shiloh (also known as the Battle of Pittsburg Landing) was the second great clash of the war and the most bitterly fought engagement of the whole struggle. In a

Red arrows on the map of the Battle of Pittsburg Landing (Shiloh) show the direction of the Confederate assault against Union forces.

herculean effort, Johnston pulled his forces together and, with 40,000 men, suddenly struck a like number of unsuspecting Union soldiers on April 6, 1862. Johnston hoped to crush Grant before the arrival of Don Carlos Buell's 20,000 Union troops, approaching from Nashville, Tennessee. A desperate combat ensued, with Confederate assaults driving the Union forces perilously close to the river. But, at the height of success, Johnston was mortally wounded. The Southern attack then lost momentum, and Grant held on until reinforced by Buell. On the following day the Union troops counterattacked and drove the Confederates, now under Beauregard, steadily from the field, forcing them to fall back to Corinth, in northern Mississippi. Grant's victory cost him 13,047 casualties, compared with Southern losses of 10,694. Halleck then assumed personal command of the combined forces of Grant, Buell, and Pope and inched forward to Corinth, which the Confederates had evacuated on May 30. With this battle and its huge losses, the people of both the Union and the Confederacy came to realize that this war would be longer and costlier than many on either side had thought in 1861.

CHAPTER THREE

THE WAR IN 1863

The first half of 1863 was grim for the Union cause. In the East, Lee's Army of Northern Virginia experienced its greatest successes. Meanwhile, Union armies in the West were stifled, especially in their efforts to take Vicksburg, Mississippi. Catastrophic Confederate losses in early July, however, left Lee unable to ever take the offensive again, gave the Union control of the Mississippi River from top to bottom, and divided the Confederacy in half. Nevertheless, problems plagued both sides as the war's toll weighed increasingly on the people at home.

THE WAR IN THE EAST

In the East, after both armies had spent the winter in camp, the arrival of the active 1863 campaign season was eagerly awaited—especially by Hooker. "Fighting Joe" had capably reorganized and refitted his army, the morale of which was high once again. The massive Army

PHOTOGRAPHY

Photography had existed for about 20 years before the war broke out, but technological developments in the late 1850s allowed for the mass production of images. More than a million tintypes, which were printed on metal, and ambrotypes, which were printed on glass, would be made during the war. Cartes de visite, a forerunner of sorts to trading cards, featured images of famous military and political figures and other celebrities, such as actors, as well as ordinary soldiers and civilians. But the most dramatic development in the field of photography was an exhibit Mathew Brady mounted in October 1862. Featuring pictures of the aftermath of Antietam, the show attracted huge crowds to Brady's New York City studio, and lines wrapped around the block. Americans had never seen photographs of such carnage before. "Mr. Brady has done something to bring home to us the terrible reality and earnestness of war. If he has not brought bodies and laid them in our dooryards and along the streets, he has done something very like it," the *New York Times* reported.

Photographer Alexander Gardner of Mathew Brady's studio took this picture of President Lincoln (center) during a visit to the Antietam battlefield in 1862.

of the Potomac numbered around 132,000 — the larg-
est army formed during the war—and was termed by
Hooker "the finest army on the planet." It was opposed
by Lee with about 62,000 troops. Hooker decided
to move most of his army up the Rappahannock,
cross, and come in upon the Confederate rear at
Fredericksburg, while John Sedgwick's smaller force
would press Lee in front.

CHANCELLORSVILLE

Beginning his turning movement on April 27, 1863,
Hooker masterfully swung around toward the west of
the Confederate army. Thus far he had outmaneuvered
Lee, but Hooker was astonished on May 1 when the
Confederate commander left a small part of his force
in Fredericksburg and suddenly moved the bulk of his
army directly against him. "Fighting Joe" lost his nerve
and pulled back to Chancellorsville, Virginia, in the
area of dense thickets called the Wilderness, where the
superior Union artillery could not be used effectively.

Lee followed up on May 2 by splitting his army
and sending Jackson on a brilliant flanking movement against Hooker's exposed right. Bursting like a
thunderbolt upon Oliver O. Howard's XI Corps late
in the afternoon, Jackson crushed this wing. While
scouting the Union forces that night, however, Jackson
was accidentally shot by his own soldiers, and he died
of complications several days later. Lee resumed the
attack on the morning of May 3 and slowly pushed

General Stonewall Jackson (left) and General Robert E. Lee meet for the last time at Chancellorsville. The Battle of Chancellorsville was one of Lee's greatest victories, but Jackson was wounded by one of his own men and died eight days later.

back Hooker, who was knocked insensible by Southern artillery fire but refused to surrender his command even temporarily. That afternoon Sedgwick drove Jubal Early's Southerners from Marye's Heights at Fredericksburg, but Lee countermarched his weary troops, fell upon Sedgwick at Salem Church, and forced him back to the north bank of the Rappahannock. Lee then returned to Chancellorsville to resume the main engagement, but Hooker, though he had 37,000 fresh troops available, gave up the contest on May 5 and retreated across the river to his old position opposite Fredericksburg. The Union suffered 17,278 casualties at Chancellorsville, while the Confederates lost 12,764.

It was a tremendous victory for Lee. His actions—splitting his force twice in the face of an adversary double his size—are still studied in military academies for their vision and audacity. Lee emerged from the battle believing that his army, even without Jackson, was invincible, and his men emerged from the fight believing that they were invincible as long as Lee was their commander. Lee's stunning success at Chancellorsville laid the groundwork for his second invasion of the North and some of the fateful decisions he would make at Gettysburg.

General Robert E. Lee rode his gray horse Traveller in many battles. After Chancellorsville, Lee believed that his army was unbeatable.

GETTYSBURG

While both armies were licking their wounds and reorganizing, Hooker, Lincoln, and Halleck debated Union strategy. They were thus engaged when Lee headed north again on June 5, 1863. What his ultimate target may have been remains a historical mystery; he never told anyone. His advance elements moved down the Shenandoah Valley toward Harpers Ferry, brushing aside small Union forces near Winchester. Marching through Maryland into Pennsylvania, the Confederates reached Chambersburg and turned eastward. They occupied York and Carlisle and menaced Harrisburg. Meanwhile, the dashing Confederate cavalryman J.E.B. ("Jeb") Stuart set off on a questionable weeklong ride around the Union army and was unable to join Lee's main army until the second day at Gettysburg.

Hooker—on unfriendly terms with Lincoln and especially Halleck—moved the Union forces northward, keeping between Lee's army and Washington. Reaching Frederick, Hooker requested that the nearly 10,000-man Union garrison at Harpers Ferry be added to his field army. When Halleck refused, Hooker resigned his command and was succeeded on June 28 by the steady George Gordon Meade, the commander of V Corps. Meade was granted a greater degree of freedom of movement than Hooker had enjoyed, and he carefully felt his way northward, looking for the Confederates.

Learning to his surprise the same day that Meade took command that the Union army was north of the Potomac, Lee hastened to concentrate his far-flung legions. Hostile forces met unexpectedly at the important crossroads town of Gettysburg, in southern Pennsylvania, bringing on the greatest battle ever fought in the Western Hemisphere. Attacking on July 1 from the west and north with 28,000 men, Confederate forces finally prevailed after nine hours of desperate fighting against 18,000 Union soldiers under John F. Reynolds. When Reynolds was killed, Abner Doubleday handled the outnumbered Union troops, but the weight of Confederate numbers forced him back through the streets of Gettysburg to strategic Cemetery Ridge south of town, where Meade assembled the rest of the army that night.

On the second day of battle, Meade's 93,000 troops were ensconced in a strong, fishhook-shaped defensive position running northward from the Round Top hills along Cemetery Ridge and then eastward around Culp's Hill. Lee, with 75,000 troops, ordered James Longstreet to attack the Union forces diagonally from Little Round Top northward and Richard S. Ewell to assail Cemetery Hill and Culp's Hill. The Confederate attack, coming in the late afternoon and evening, saw Longstreet capture the positions known as the Peach Orchard, Wheat Field, and Devil's Den on the Union left in furious fighting but fail to seize the vital Little Round Top. Ewell's later assaults on Cemetery Hill were repulsed, and he could capture only a part of Culp's Hill.

On the morning of the third day, Meade's right wing drove the Confederates from the lower slopes of Culp's Hill and checked Stuart's cavalry sweep to the east of Gettysburg in midafternoon. Then, in what has been called the greatest infantry charge in American history,

Confederate General George E. Pickett's charge on July 3, 1863, during the Battle of Gettysburg, was a climactic attack on Cemetery Ridge. The Confederates broke through Union defenses, but they had to retreat. Fewer than one-fourth of Pickett's men returned.

Lee—against Longstreet's advice—hurled nearly 15,000 soldiers under the command of Generals George E. Pickett, J. Johnston Pettigrew, and Isaac R. Trimble against the center of Meade's lines on Cemetery Ridge, following a fearful and deafening artillery duel of two hours. Despite heroic efforts, only several hundred Southerners temporarily breached the low rock wall at the center of the Union forces. The rest were shot down by Union cannoneers and riflemen, captured, or

The dedication ceremony for the National Cemetery at Gettysburg Battlefield was held on November 9, 1863. President Abraham Lincoln, hatless, is seated left of center. He delivered the famous Gettysburg Address at the ceremony.

thrown back, suffering casualties of almost 60 percent. To Lincoln's great consternation, Meade felt unable to counterattack, and Lee retreated into Virginia. The Confederacy had lost 28,063 men at Gettysburg and the Union had lost 23,049.

After indecisive maneuvering and light actions in northern Virginia in the fall of 1863, the two armies went into winter quarters. Lee's decisions on the third day have long been the subject of debate but are best understood in the context of coming just a few weeks after his greatest victory, at Chancellorsville. But the consequences of Gettysburg, while not ultimately decisive, were catastrophic nonetheless. Lee had lost a number of his hardened veterans along with many of his generals and colonels, and they could not be replaced. Never again would Lee be able to mount a full-scale invasion of the North with his entire army. Instead, he would have to spend the rest of the war on the defensive.

THE WAR IN THE WEST

The surrender of Vicksburg was an important victory for the Union. It was one of several significant turning points in the war but was not decisive on its own. Confederate troops continued to put up a considerable fight, defeating Union forces at Chickamauga Creek, Georgia, and imposing great suffering at Chattanooga before finally losing that city.

ARKANSAS AND VICKSBURG

In Arkansas, Union troops under General Frederick Steele moved upon the Confederates and defeated them at Prairie Grove, near Fayetteville, on December 7, 1862—a victory that paved the way for Steele's eventual capture of Little Rock the next September.

More important, Grant, back in good graces following his undistinguished performance at Shiloh, was authorized to move against the Confederate "Gibraltar of the West"—Vicksburg, Mississippi. This bastion was difficult to approach: Admiral David Farragut, Grant, and Sherman had failed to capture it in 1862. In the early months of 1863, in the so-called Bayou Expeditions, Grant was again frustrated in his efforts to get at Vicksburg from the north.

Finally, escorted by Admiral David Dixon Porter's gunboats, which ran the Confederate batteries at Vicksburg, Grant landed his army to the south at Bruinsburg, Mississippi, on April 30, 1863, and pressed northeastward. He won small but sharp actions at Port Gibson, Raymond, and Jackson, while the circumspect Confederate defender of Vicksburg, John C. Pemberton, was unable to link up with a smaller Southern force under Joseph E. Johnston near Jackson.

Turning due westward toward the rear of Vicksburg's defenses, Grant overwhelmed Pemberton's army at Champion's Hill and the Big Black River and enveloped the town. During his 47-day siege, Grant eventually had an army of 71,000; Pemberton's command numbered 31,000, of whom 18,500 were effectives (soldiers equipped for duty). The outnumbered and starving Confederates were forced to surrender on July 4. Five days later, 6,000 rebels yielded to Nathaniel P. Banks at Port Hudson, Louisiana, to the south of Vicksburg and one of the last Confederate strongholds on the Mississippi, a loss that divided the Confederacy in half.

CHICKAMAUGA AND CHATTANOOGA

Meanwhile, 60,000 Union soldiers under William S. Rosecrans sought to move southeastward from central Tennessee against the important Confederate rail and industrial center of Chattanooga, then held by Braxton Bragg with some 43,000 troops. In a series of brilliantly conceived movements, Rosecrans maneuvered Bragg out of Chattanooga without having to fight a battle. Bragg was then bolstered by troops from Longstreet's veteran corps, sent swiftly by rail from Lee's army in

Union army engineers rebuild the Tennessee River Bridge at Chattanooga, Tennessee, in 1863. The North's victory in the Battle of Chattanooga gave the Union control of the railroads centered in Chattanooga.

Virginia. With this reinforcement, Bragg turned on Rosecrans and—in a vicious two-day battle (September 19–20) at Chickamauga Creek, just southeast of Chattanooga—gained one of the few Confederate victories in the West. Bragg lost 18,454 of his 66,326 men; Rosecrans, 16,170 out of 53,919 engaged. Rosecrans fell back into Chattanooga, where he was almost encircled by Bragg. Bragg was able to choke off supplies to the point that Union troops were starving.

But the Southern success was short-lived. Instead of pressing the siege of Chattanooga, Bragg unwisely

sent Longstreet off in a futile attempt to capture Knoxville, then being held by Burnside. When Rosecrans showed signs of disintegration, Lincoln replaced him with Grant, who was able to establish a supply line by late October and strengthened the hard-pressed Union army at Chattanooga by sending, by rail, the remnants of the Army of the

Potomac's XI and XII Corps, under Hooker's command. Outnumbering Bragg now 56,359 to 46,165, Grant attacked on November 23–25, capturing Lookout Mountain and Missionary Ridge, defeating Bragg's army, and driving it southward toward Dalton, Georgia. Grant sustained 5,824 casualties at Chattanooga and Bragg, 6,667. Confidence having been lost in Bragg by most of his top generals, Davis replaced him with Johnston. Both armies remained inactive until the following spring.

THE WAR IN 1864–65

Finally dissatisfied with Halleck as general in chief and impressed with Grant's victories, Lincoln appointed Grant to supersede Halleck and to assume the rank of lieutenant general, which Congress had re-created. Leaving Sherman in command in the West, Grant arrived in Washington on March 8, 1864. He was given largely a free hand in developing his grand strategy. He retained Meade in technical command of the Army of the Potomac but in effect assumed direct control by establishing his own headquarters with it. He sought to move this army against Lee in northern Virginia while Sherman marched against Johnston and Atlanta. Several lesser Union armies were also to advance in May.

GRANT'S OVERLAND CAMPAIGN

Grant surged across the Rapidan and Rappahannock rivers in Virginia on May 4, hoping to get through the tangled Wilderness before Lee could move. But the Confederate leader reacted instantly and, on May 5, attacked Grant from the west in the Battle of the Wilderness. Two days of bitter, indecisive combat ensued. Although Grant had 115,000 men available against Lee's 62,000, he found both Union flanks endangered. Moreover, Grant lost 17,666 soldiers, compared with a probable Southern loss of about 8,000. Pulling away from the Wilderness battlefield, Grant tried to hasten southeastward to the crossroads point of Spotsylvania Court House, only to have the Confederates get there first. In savage action (May 8–19), including hand-to-hand fighting at the famous "Bloody Angle," Grant, although gaining a little ground, was essentially thrown back. He had lost 18,399 men at Spotsylvania. Lee's combined losses at the Wilderness and Spotsylvania were an estimated 17,250.

Again Grant withdrew, only to move forward in another series of attempts to get past Lee's right flank. Again, at the North Anna River and at Totopotomoy Creek, he found Lee confronting him. Finally, at Cold Harbor, just northeast of Richmond, Grant launched several heavy attacks, including a frontal, nearly suicidal one on June 3, only to be repelled with grievous total losses of 12,737. Lee's casualties are unknown but were much lighter.

Grant, with the vital rail center of Petersburg—the southern key to Richmond—as his objective, made one final effort to swing around Lee's right and finally outguessed his opponent and stole a march on him.

General Ulysses S. Grant was named commander in chief of all Union armies in March 1864. He is seen here at his headquarters in Cold Harbor, Virginia, in June 1864, during the last battle of his Overland Campaign.

But several blunders by Union officers, swift action by Beauregard, and Lee's belated though rapid reaction enabled the Confederates to hold Petersburg. Grant attacked on June 15 and 18, hoping to break through before Lee could consolidate the Confederate lines east of the city, but he was contained with 8,150 losses.

Unable to admit defeat but having failed to destroy Lee's army and capture Richmond, Grant settled down to a nine-month active siege of Petersburg. The summer and fall of 1864 were highlighted by the Union failure with a mine explosion under Confederate lines at Petersburg on July 30 (the Battle of the Crater), the near capture of Washington by the Confederate Jubal Early in July, and Early's later setbacks in the Shenandoah Valley at the hands of Philip H. Sheridan.

Petersburg was a strategic point for the defense of the Confederate capital of Richmond. When Petersburg fell to the Union in April 1865, Lee had to evacuate and head west.

THE MARCH TO THE SEA

Sherman's March to the Sea marked a new development in the war. To this point, Union armies had generally avoided targeting civilians and their property other than slaves. Sherman had decided, though, that he had to crush the will of white Southern civilians if the Union were to bring the rebels to heel. He promised to "make Georgia howl," and he did. His men destroyed everything of military value that they encountered, including railroads, telegraph lines, and warehouses. They were trailed by foragers, stragglers, deserters, Georgia militiamen, and some Confederate cavalry who committed a variety of depredations on the population, including pillaging and burning civilian property. Sherman was blamed not only for his own actions but also for the actions of others not necessarily under his control. Nevertheless, Sherman himself reported that his men had racked up $100 million in damage to Georgia, 80 percent of which was "simple waste and destruction" and the remainder being straightforward military targets.

In Sherman's March to the Sea, Union troops cut a wide swath as they moved south through Georgia, destroying railroads and supplies, reducing the war-making potential of the Confederacy, and bringing the war home to the Southern civilians.

SHERMAN'S GEORGIA AND CAROLINA CAMPAIGNS

Meanwhile, Sherman was pushing off toward Atlanta on May 7, 1864. His 110,123 men engaged Confederates under General Joseph Johnston and later General John B. Hood. After a series of Union assaults were thwarted, Sherman's Army of the West captured Atlanta on September 2, 1864. On November 15 he began his great March to the Sea with 62,000 men, laying waste to the economic resources of Georgia in a 50-mile- (80-kilometer-) wide swath of destruction. He captured Savannah, 285 miles (460 kilometers) from Atlanta, on December 21. Meanwhile General Hood, attempting a counterattack in Tennessee, was decisively defeated at Franklin on November 30 and at Nashville on December 15–16.

On January 10, 1865, with Tennessee and Georgia now securely in Union hands, Sherman's force began to march northward into the Carolinas. It was only lightly opposed by much smaller Confederate forces. Sherman's men blamed South Carolina for bringing on the war and sought to punish them for their actions. What had happened in Georgia paled in comparison with the devastation the Northerners wrought in South Carolina. Once again, civilians were not killed, but the Union troops did everything they could to demoralize the population and undermine their support for the war. Sherman captured Columbia, South Carolina, on February 17 and compelled the Confederates to evacuate Charleston (including

William Tecumseh Sherman led Union forces in crushing campaigns through the South. He was a master of modern warfare.

Fort Sumter). When Lee was finally named Confederate general in chief, he promptly reinstated Johnston as commander of the small forces striving to oppose the Union advance. Nonetheless, Sherman pushed on into North Carolina, capturing Fayetteville on March 11 and, after an initial setback, repulsing the counterattacking Johnston at Bentonville on March 19–20. Goldsboro fell to the Union on March 23 and Raleigh on April 13. Finally, perceiving that he no longer had any reasonable chance of containing the relentless Union advance, Johnston surrendered to Sherman at the Bennett House near Durham Station on April 18. When Sherman's generous terms proved unacceptable to Secretary of War Stanton (Lincoln had been assassinated on April 14), the former submitted new terms that Johnston signed on April 26.

THE FINAL LAND OPERATIONS

Grant and Meade were continuing their siege of Petersburg and Richmond early in 1865. For months the Union forces had been lengthening their left (southern) flank while operating against several important railroads supplying the two Confederate cities. This stretched Lee's dwindling forces very thin. The Southern leader briefly threatened to break the siege when he attacked and captured Fort Stedman (near Petersburg) on March 25. But an immediate Union counterattack regained the strongpoint, and Lee, when his lines were subsequently pierced, evacuated both

Petersburg and Richmond on the night of April 2–3.

An 88-mile (142-kilometer) pursuit west-south-westward along the Appomattox River in Virginia ensued, with Grant and Meade straining every nerve to bring Lee to bay. The Confederates were detained at Amelia Court House, awaiting delayed food supplies, and were badly beaten at Five Forks and Sayler's Creek, with their only avenue of escape now cut off by Sheridan and George A. Custer. When Lee's final attempt to break out failed, he surrendered the remnants of his Army of Northern Virginia at Appomattox Court House on April 9.

On the outskirts of the Confederacy, 43,000 Confederates in Louisiana under E. Kirby Smith surrendered to Edward Canby on May 26. The port of Galveston, Texas, yielded to the Union on June 2, and the greatest war on American soil was over.

CONCLUSION

Although the Civil War preserved the Union, the physical, psychological, and economic costs were enormous. While desertions plagued both sides during the war, the personal valor and the enormous casualties have not yet ceased to astound scholars and military historians. Based on the three-year standard of enlistment, about 1,556,000 soldiers served in the Union armies, and about 800,000 men probably served in the Confederate forces, though spotty records make it impossible to know for sure. Traditionally, historians have put war deaths at about 360,000 for the Union and 260,000 for the Confederates. In the second decade of the 21st century, however, a demographer used better data and more sophisticated tools to convincingly revise the total death toll upward to 752,000 and indicated that it could be as high as 851,000. More Americans died in the Civil War than in World War I, World War II, the Korean War, and the Vietnam War combined.

It is often said that the Civil War tragically pitted "brother against brother." This image works as a metaphor for the terrible divisiveness of the conflict, representing the country as a family. It was also literally true. In many American families—especially in the upper South, or border states—some family members openly sympathized with the South, while other members publicly sided with the North. In some cases, brothers or other family members actually fought on opposing sides in the war. President Lincoln himself had brothers-in-law who fought for the Confederacy.

The war was also very costly economically. Faced with a shortage of funds, both governments were obliged to print large amounts of paper money. As a result, both sides experienced runaway inflation. Inflation was much more drastic in the South, where,

Union soldiers are photographed outside the McLean House at Appomattox Court House, Virginia, in April 1865. There General Lee surrendered to General Grant, effectively ending the Ciivl War.

by the end of the war, flour sold at $1,000 a barrel. While separate Confederate figures are lacking, the war finally cost the United States more than $15 billion. The South, especially, where most of the war was fought and which lost its labor system, was physically and economically devastated. Some spiritual wounds caused by the war still have not been healed.

1750 The legal establishment of slavery occurs in all English colonies in the New World.

1775–83 The 13 North American colonies fight the American Revolution to win independence from Great Britain.

1774–1804 Slavery is abolished in the Northern states, but it remains essential to the South.

1776 In the Declaration of Independence, a passage that condemned the slave trade is removed because of political pressure from the Southern colonies.

1788 The U.S. Constitution is ratified and allows for the continuation of the slave trade for another 20 years. It also requires states to assist slaveholders in the recovery of fugitive slaves and specifies that a slave counts as three-fifths of a person for the purposes of taxation and for determining representation in the House of Representatives.

1807–08 The U.S. Congress bans the African slave trade in 1807, which takes effect in January 1808.

1820 Congress passes the Missouri Compromise, allowing Missouri to join the Union as a slave state. Maine had earlier entered the Union as a free state.

1850 The Compromise of 1850 tries to maintain an even balance between the number of free and slave states in the Union.

1854 Congress passes the Kansas-Nebraska Act, which repeals the Missouri Compromise. The act creates

Kansas and Nebraska as territories and allows the people of each territory to decide for themselves whether or not to allow slavery.

1860 Abraham Lincoln is elected president of the United States. On December 20, South Carolina secedes from the Union.

February 1861 The Confederate States of America is established, and Jefferson Davis becomes president.

April 12, 1861 Confederate troops under General P.G.T. Beauregard attack Fort Sumter in Charleston, South Carolina, beginning the Civil War.

July 21, 1861 Union forces under General Irvin McDowell are defeated in the First Battle of Bull Run.

November 1861 Lincoln appoints George B. McClellan as commander of all Union forces, replacing Winfield Scott.

February 1862 Union General Ulysses S. Grant captures Fort Henry and Fort Donelson in Tennessee.

March 9, 1862 The Confederate ironclad *Merrimack* battles the Union ironclad *Monitor* to a draw.

April 4, 1862 McClellan begins the Peninsular Campaign.

April 6–7, 1862 Both sides suffer heavy losses in the Battle of Shiloh.

June 1862 General Robert E. Lee takes command of Confederate forces and renames them the Army of Northern Virginia.

July 1862 President Lincoln names General Henry W. Halleck as commander of Union forces.

August 29–30, 1862 Union General John Pope is defeated by Confederate Generals Stonewall Jackson and James Longstreet at the Second Battle of Bull Run.

September 17, 1862 General Lee and his Confederate troops fight General McClellan and his Union troops at the Battle of Antietam in Maryland.

November 1862 President Lincoln relieves McClellan of his command and chooses General Ambrose Burnside to lead the Army of the Potomac.

December 13, 1862 General Burnside and his forces are defeated at the Battle of Fredericksburg in Virginia.

January 1, 1863 President Lincoln issues the Emancipation Proclamation, which freed all slaves in the Confederate states and territories.

January 25, 1863 General Joseph Hooker becomes commander of the Army of the Potomac.

January 29, 1863 General Grant becomes commander of the Army of the West and receives orders to capture Vicksburg.

May 1–4, 1863 General Hooker is defeated by General Lee at the Battle of Chancellorsville in Virginia. General Stonewall Jackson is seriously wounded and dies on May 10.

June 28, 1863 President Lincoln names General George G. Meade as commander of the Army of the Potomac.

July 1–3, 1863 Union forces defeat General Lee and his Confederates in the Battle of Gettysburg.

July 4, 1863 General Grant takes Vicksburg, dividing the Confederacy.

September 19–20, 1863 General Braxton Bragg's Confederates defeat General William Rosecrans and his Union troops at Chickamauga.

November 23–25, 1863 General Grant defeats General Bragg at Chattanooga.

March 9, 1864 Grant becomes commander of all Union forces.

May 5–7, 1864 Forces led by Grant and Lee fight the intense but indecisive Battle of the Wilderness.

May 8–19, 1864 Grant and Lee battle at Spotsylvania.

September 2, 1864 General William T. Sherman captures Atlanta.

November 15, 1864 Sherman begins his March to the Sea. He would capture Savannah on December 21.

April 2–3, 1865 Lee evacuates both Petersburg and Richmond.

April 9, 1865 Grant accepts Lee's surrender at Appomattox Court House, Virginia.

April 14, 1865 Abraham Lincoln is assassinated.

May 1865 The remaining Confederate forces surrender, ending the Civil War.

December 6, 1865 The Thirteenth Amendment to the U.S. Constitution is ratified, abolishing slavery.

GLOSSARY

abolish To officially end or stop.

ambrotype A positive picture made on glass and viewed against a dark background.

blockade The cutting off of an area by means of troops or warships to stop the coming in or going out of people or supplies.

carte de visite A calling card, especially one with a photographic portrait mounted on it, that was hugely popular in the mid–19th century.

compromise A settlement of a dispute that involves each party giving up some demands.

conscription A forced enrollment of people into the military; draft.

demographer A person who specializes in the statistical study of characteristics of human populations, such as size and density, distribution, and vital statistics.

demoralize To cause someone to lose hope, courage, or confidence.

emancipation The act of freeing someone from slavery.

hypersensitivity The state of being excessively sensitive to something

ironclad A type of warship of the 19th century with iron casemates that protected the hull.

micromanage To try to control or manage all the small parts of something, such as an activity, in a way that is usually not wanted or that causes problems.

morality Beliefs about what is right behavior and what is wrong behavior.

ordnance Military supplies or artillery.

per capita Per unit of population: by or for each person.

proclamation Something that is announced publicly or declared formally.

repulse To drive back or repel.

rout A disastrous defeat.

secede To separate from a nation or state and become independent.

writ of habeas corpus An essential safeguard of personal liberty; an order to bring a jailed person before a judge or court to find out if that person should really be in jail.

FOR MORE INFORMATION

Abraham Lincoln Presidential Library and Museum
212 North 6th Street
Springfield, IL 62701
(217) 558-8844
Website: http://www.illinois.gov/alplm
Lincoln's presidential library and museum holds exten-
sive documents and records relating to his personal
life and presidency.

African American Civil War Memorial & Museum
1925 Vermont Avenue NW
Washington, DC 20011
(202) 667-2667
Website: http://www.afroamcivilwar.org
This memorial honors the service of African American
soldiers and sailors who fought for the Union.

Civil War Trust
Civil War Trust Corporate Office
1156 15th Street NW, Suite 900
Washington, DC 20005
(202) 367-1861
Website: http://www.civilwar.org
This organization works to preserve and protect Civil
War battlefields and offers programs to the pub-
lic about the history of the battles, including Fort
Sumter, Shiloh, Antietam, and Gettysburg.

National Civil War Museum
One Lincoln Circle at Reservoir Park
Harrisburg, PA 17103
(717) 260-1861
Website: http://www.nationalcivilwarmuseum.org
Exhibits that include artifacts, documents, and photo-
    graphs concerning Civil War battles can be viewed
    in this museum.

National Museum of Civil War Medicine
P.O. Box 470
48 East Patrick Street
Frederick, MD 21705
(301) 695-1864
Website: http://www.civilwarmed.org
The museum was created in 1990 to exhibit medical
    artifacts from the Civil War and now includes the Pry
    House Field Hospital Museum and the Clara Barton
    Missing Soldiers Office. Its research center offers a
    wealth of material on Civil War medicine.

National Park Service
U.S. Department of the Interior
Civil War Monuments
Website: http://www.nps.gov/civilwar/search-
    monuments.htm
The National Park Service manages many Civil War
    battlefields, monuments, and memorials. You can
    search for monuments by state, by battle unit name,
    or by park.

Sons of Union Veterans of the Civil War
1 Lincoln Circle at Reservoir Park, Suite 240
Harrisburg, PA 17103-2411
(717) 232-7000
Website: http://www.suvcw.org
This group is dedicated to preserving the history and
legacy of people who fought for the Union in the
Civil War.

WEBSITES

Because of the changing nature of Internet links, Rosen
Publishing has developed an online list of websites
related to the subject of this book. This site is updated
regularly. Please use this link to access the list:

http://www.rosenlinks.com/EAH/Civil

BIBLIOGRAPHY

Ashworth, John. *The Republic in Crisis, 1848–1861*. New York, NY: Cambridge University Press, 2012.

Bailey, Diane. *The Emancipation Proclamation and the End of Slavery in America* (A Celebration of the Civil Rights Movement). New York, NY: Rosen Publishing Group, 2015.

Baptiste, Tracey, ed. *The Civil War and Reconstruction Eras* (The African American Experience: From Slavery to the Presidency). New York, NY: Britannica Educational Publishing and Rosen Educational Services, 2015.

The Civil War: A Visual History. Revised edition. New York, NY: DK Publishing, 2015.

Field, Ron. *Robert E. Lee*. Oxford, England: Osprey Publishing, 2010.

Garrison, Webb B. *Brady's Civil War: A Collection of Memorable Civil War Images Photographed by Matthew Brady and His Assistants.* Revised edition. New York, NY: Lyons Press, 2011.

Hettle, Wallace. *Inventing Stonewall Jackson: A Civil War Hero in History and Memory*. Baton Rouge, LA: Louisiana State University Press, 2011.

Hollar, Sherman, ed. *Biographies of the Civil War and Reconstruction: Abraham Lincoln, Robert E. Lee, Ulysses S. Grant, and More* (Impact on America: Collective Biographies). New York, NY: Britannica Educational Publishing and Rosen Educational Services, 2013.

Kagan, Neil, and Stephen G. Hyslop. *Atlas of the Civil War: A Comprehensive Guide to the Tactics and Terrain of Battle*. Washington, D.C.: National Geographic Society, 2009.

Kalasky, Robert J. *Shadows of Antietam*. Kent, OH: Kent State University Press, 2012.

Marcello, Paul, and Rob Morris. *The Civil War Close Up* (The War Chronicles). New York, NY: Rosen Publishing, 2016.

Nardo, Don. *Slavery Through the Ages* (World History). Detroit, MI: Lucent Books, 2014.

O'Neill, Robert, ed. *The Civil War: Bull Run and Other Eastern Battles 1861–May 1863* (The Civil War: Essential Histories). New York, NY: Rosen Publishing, 2011.

O'Neill, Robert, ed. *The Civil War: Gettysburg and Other Eastern Battles 1863–1865* (The Civil War: Essential Histories). New York, NY: Rosen Publishing, 2011.

O'Neill, Robert, ed. *The Civil War: Sherman's Capture of Atlanta and Other Western Battles 1863–1865* (The Civil War: Essential Histories). New York, NY: Rosen Publishing, 2011.

O'Neill, Robert, ed. *The Civil War: The Siege of Vicksburg and Other Western Battles, 1861–July 1863* (The Civil War: Essential Histories). New York, NY: Rosen Publishing, 2011.

Rogers, Clifford J. *The West Point History of the Civil War*. New York, NY: Simon & Schuster, 2014.

Trudeau, Noah Andre. *Southern Storm: Sherman's March to the Sea*. New York, NY: Harper Perennial, 2009.

INDEX

A

American Revolution, 14
Anaconda Plan, 17
Anderson, Robert, 10
Antietam, 29, 31, 32–33, 40
Appomattox Court House, 63
Army of Northern Virginia, 28, 39, 63
Army of the Potomac, 23, 28, 31, 34, 40–41, 51– 52, 53

B

Bayou Expeditions, 49
Beauregard, P.G.T., 10, 20, 21, 38, 56
Black Hawk War, 15
border states, 19, 35, 64
Brady, Mathew, 40
Bragg, Braxton, 50–52
Buell, Don Carlos, 48
Bull Run (Manassas)
    first battle of, 21–23
    second battle of, 29–31
Burnside, Ambrose E., 33, 34, 51

C

Cameron, Simon, 15
Chancellorsville, 41–43, 48
Chattanooga, 48, 50–52
Chickamauga, 48, 51–52

Civil War
    causes of, 8–9
    death toll of, 64
    effects of, 64–66
Cold Harbor, 54
Confederate States of America
    blockade of, 10, 12, 14, 17
    division of/loss of Mississippi River, 39, 49
    formation of, 6, 9
    surrender of, 62, 63

D

Davis, Jefferson, 12, 14–15, 16, 28, 52

E

Early, Jubal, 42, 56
Emancipation Proclamation, 31

F

Fayetteville, 48, 62
Fort Donelson, 36–37
Fort Henry, 36–37
Fort Sumter, 6, 10, 18, 62
Fredericksburg, 34, 41, 42, 43

G

Gettysburg, 43–48
Grant, Ulysses S., 23, 36, 37, 38, 48, 49, 51, 52, 53–56, 61, 62

H

Halleck, Henry, 29, 33, 36, 38, 43, 44, 53
Harpers Ferry, 20, 28, 32, 44
Hood, John B., 60
Hooker, Joseph "Fighting Joe," 34, 39, 41, 42, 43, 44, 52

I

ironclad warships, 25–27

J

Jackson, Thomas Jonathan "Stonewall," 21, 28, 29, 32, 41, 43
Johnston, Albert Sidney, 36, 37, 38
Johnston, Joseph E., 21, 24, 28, 49, 52, 53, 60, 62

L

Lee, Robert E., 15, 19, 20, 28, 29, 31, 32, 34, 39, 41, 42–44, 45, 46, 47–48, 50, 53, 54, 56, 62–63
Lincoln, Abraham, 9, 10–11, 14–15, 16, 17, 20, 24, 29, 31, 33, 34, 35, 43, 44, 47, 51, 53, 62, 65
Longstreet, James, 29, 45, 46, 50, 51

M

March to the Sea, 58, 60
McClellan, George B., 18, 20, 23–24, 28–29, 31, 32–33
McDowell, Irvin, 20, 21
Meade, George Gordon, 44, 45, 46, 47, 53, 62, 63
Merrimack, 25–27
Mexican-American War, 8, 14
Mississippi River, 17, 18, 36, 37, 39, 49
Missouri Compromise, 8
Monitor, 27

N

Norfolk naval base, 20, 25
North, the
    as compared to the South, 6–8, 12–14
    economy of, 6–7
Northwest Ordinance of 1784, 8

P

Pea Ridge (Elkhorn Tavern), 36
Pemberton, John C., 49
Peninsular Campaign, 24, 28–29
Petersburg, 54–56, 62, 63
photography, 40
Pope, John, 29, 31, 37, 38
Potomac River, 12, 32, 44

R

railroads, 7, 8, 12, 20, 50, 51, 58, 62

Rappahannock River, 29, 34, 41, 42, 53
Richmond, 19, 20, 28, 29, 54, 55, 62, 63
Rosecrans, William S., 50, 51

S

Scott, Winfield, 17, 20, 23
Sedgwick, John, 41, 42
Seven Days' Battles, 28
Seven Pines, 28
Shenandoah Valley, 21, 28, 44, 56
Sheridan, Philip H., 56, 63
Sherman, William T., 37, 49, 53, 58, 60, 62
Shiloh (Pittsburg Landing), 37, 48
slavery, 6, 8, 9, 12
Spotsylvania, 54
South, the
    as compared to the North, 6–8, 12–14
    economy of, 8
    effects of losing the Civil War, 65–66
    industrial weakness of, 14
    secession of, 6, 9, 12, 20
Stanton, Edwin M., 15, 24, 62
Steele, Frederick, 48
Stuart, J.E.B. ("Jeb"), 44, 45

V

Vicksburg, 39, 48, 49

W

Washington, D.C., 20, 21, 23, 24, 29, 44, 53, 56
West Virginia, secession from Confederacy and admittance to Union, 20
Wilderness, 41, 54
Wilson's Creek, 36